ANIMALS THAT DIG

Angela Royston

raintree
a Capstone company — publishers for children

Raintree is an imprint of Capstone Global Library Limited, a company incorporated in England and Wales having its registered office at 7 Pilgrim Street, London, EC4V 6LB – Registered company number: 6695582

www.raintreepublishers.co.uk
myorders@raintreepublishers.co.uk

Text © Capstone Global Library Limited 2014
First published in hardback in 2014
Paperback edition first published in 2015
The moral rights of the proprietor have been asserted.

Edited by Dan Nunn, Rebecca Rissman, and Helen Cox Cannons
Designed by Jo Hinton-Malivoire
Picture research by Mica Brancic
Originated by Capstone Global Library Ltd
Production by Helen McCreath
Printed and bound in China

ISBN 978 1 406 27083 9 (hardback)
17 16 15 14 13
10 9 8 7 6 5 4 3 2 1

ISBN 978 1 406 27090 7 (paperback)
18 17 16 15 14
10 9 8 7 6 5 4 3 2 1

British Library Cataloguing in Publication Data
A full catalogue record for this book is available from the British Library.

Acknowledgements
We would like to thank the following for permission to reproduce photographs: FLPA pp. 15 (Minden Pictures/Pete Oxford), 16 (Frans Lanting), 21 (Minden Pictures/Kevin Schafer), 23 (Minden Pictures/Oliver Lucanus), 24 (Photo Researchers); Naturepl.com pp. 4, 12 (© Ingo Arndt), 7 (© Ashish & Shanthi Chandola), 8 (© Edwin Giesbers), 9 (© Ann & Steve Toon), 11 (© George McCarthy), 13 (© David Welling), 14 (© Dave Watts), 17 (© Andy Rouse), 18 (© Steven Kazlowski), 19 (© Eric Baccega), 26 (© Philippe Clement), 27 (ARCO/© Meul); Shutterstock pp. 5 (© Yory Frenklakh), 29 top right (© Marcin Pawinski), 29 top left (© Bplanet), 29 bottom right (© Henrik Larsson), 29 bottom left (© Jo Crebbin); SuperStock pp. 6 (Minden Pictures), 10 (imagebroker.net), 20 (All Canada Photos/Tim Zurowski), 22 (Minden Pictures), 25 (All Canada Photos/Wayne Lynch).

Cover photograph of a mole (*Talpa occidentalis*) emerging from its burrow reproduced with permission of Getty Images (Taxi/Timelaps/Tony Evans).

We would like to thank Michael Bright for his invaluable help in the preparation of this book.

Every effort has been made to contact copyright holders of material reproduced in this book. Any omissions will be rectified in subsequent printings if notice is given to the publisher.

Disclaimer
All the internet addresses (URLs) given in this book were valid at the time of going to press. However, due to the dynamic nature of the internet, some addresses may have changed, or sites may have changed or ceased to exist since publication. While the author and publisher regret any inconvenience this may cause readers, no responsibility for any such changes can be accepted by either the author or the publisher.

Some words are shown in bold, **like this**. You can find out what they mean by looking in the glossary.

CONTENTS

Good at digging 4

Digging to survive 6

Adapted to dig 8

Moles 10

Prairie dogs 12

Wombats 14

Tusks 16

Polar bears. 18

Armadillos .20

Gila monsters. 22

Spadefoot toads 24

Earthworms 26

Animal challenge 28

Glossary 30

Find out more 31

Index 32

GOOD AT DIGGING

Many different kinds of animal dig into the ground. Large grizzly bears and tiny beetles are both good at digging. Digging animals live almost everywhere – from the icy Arctic to the hottest deserts. What makes them such good diggers?

beetle

A black beetle uses its six legs to dig through hot desert sand to reach cooler sand below.

DIGGING TO SURVIVE

Digging helps animals **survive**. Some animals dig to find food. Meerkats and other animals dig underground **burrows** where they are safe from **predators**.

meerkats

Indian desert gerbil

Stay cool!
Deserts are very hot during the day and cold at night. Many desert animals live below ground where it is neither too hot nor too cold.

ADAPTED TO DIG

Adaptations are special things about an animal's body that help it to **survive**. Many digging animals, such as the coati, have strong legs and sharp claws. An American badger is one of the fastest digging animals. Its front claws are sharp, long, and strong.

A coati pushes its long nose through leaves to find food.

American badger

MOLES

Moles spend almost all their lives below ground. They have strong legs and large feet with powerful claws – perfect for digging tunnels! Their long, thin bodies and short legs make it easy for them to wriggle through tunnels to find worms and other food.

claw

As the mole digs, it
pushes out the loose
soil to form a molehill.

PRAIRIE DOGS

Prairie dogs **burrow** into the soil in **grasslands** in North America. Their short legs, large feet, and long claws are excellent for digging. As they nibble the grass, they watch out for danger. Then they dash below ground.

Megacity
Prairie dogs live in large groups, called colonies or towns. The largest prairie dog colony ever counted had about 400 million animals!

WOMBATS

Wombats are **marsupials**, and they are well **adapted** for digging deep **burrows** with their strong legs and broad claws. Like all marsupials, a wombat mother carries her baby in a pouch, but a wombat's pouch faces backwards. This saves her baby from getting covered in soil when she digs.

pouch

baby wombat

TUSKS

A warthog is a wild pig. It uses its paws and snout to dig for roots and bulbs to eat. Its sharp tusks are an extra **adaptation** for digging.

African elephants have the longest tusks in the world – they are up to 3 metres (10 feet) long!

DID YOU KNOW?
Tusks are extra long teeth! Elephants use their tusks to dig for water and roots.

POLAR BEARS

Polar bears use their big feet and sharp claws to dig into snowdrifts or the ice. They are the biggest animals that make **burrows** or dens. Female bears dig dens in snowdrifts in winter before giving birth to cubs.

Female polar bears' icy homes keep them and their cubs warm through the Arctic winter.

ARMADILLOS

Armadillos come from South America. They use their long, tough claws to dig dens and to find grubs and roots in the soil. A giant armadillo has an extra-long middle claw on each front foot. They use these claws to dig for food and to rip into **termite** nests.

Plates of bony armour protect an armadillo's skin.

Termites are an armadillo's favourite food!

termite nest

long claw

GILA MONSTERS

Gila monsters live in deserts in Mexico and the United States. These big lizards have strong front legs and claws, which they use to dig **burrows**.

scales

claws

DID YOU KNOW?
A gila monster eats so much food in summer that its tail becomes fat. This fat keeps it going all winter, when it stays in its burrow and eats nothing.

SPADEFOOT TOADS

Spadefoot toads live in hot deserts. They get their name from hard "spades" on their back legs. These spades help them to dig deep **burrows**. Spadefoot toads spend almost all their lives underground, waiting for heavy rain. Then they come out and lay eggs in the puddles of water.

Spadefoots use their spades to burrow backwards!

spade-like back legs

DID YOU KNOW?
Spadefoot tadpoles quickly change into toads before their puddle dries up!

EARTHWORMS

An earthworm spends its whole life tunnelling through the soil. It has a long, thin body but no legs, feet, or claws. Instead, it has **bristles** that help it to grip the soil. Many earthworms have a slimy skin.

Slime factory

An earthworm's slimy skin makes it easier for the worm to slide through tunnels in the soil.

ANIMAL CHALLENGE

1. Why is a horse not very good at digging?

2. Which do you think can dig better – a cat or a dog?

3. Sea turtles bury their eggs in dry sand. Why do you think they do that?

Invent a new burrowing animal! Think about where your invented animal lives and why it digs. You can use the **adaptations** shown in the photos, or you can make up some of your own.

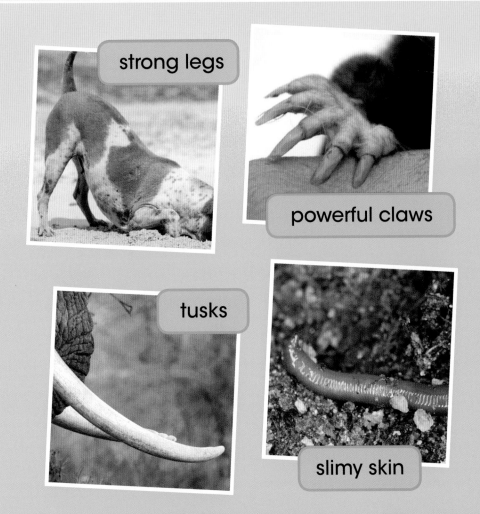

strong legs

powerful claws

tusks

slimy skin

Answers to Animal Challenge
1. A horse has smooth, rounded hooves, which are not good for digging.
2. A dog is better at digging. It uses its big front paws to scoop the soil away through its back legs.
3. Sea turtles bury their eggs to keep them safe. They choose dry sand so that the eggs will not be washed away by the waves.

GLOSSARY

adaptation special thing about an animal's body that helps it to survive in a particular way or in a particular habitat

adapted well suited to a particular activity or way of living

bristles short, stiff hairs

burrow home dug below the surface of the ground by some types of animal

grassland area where the main plants are grass and there are few trees

marsupial animal that carries its newborn baby in a pouch on the mother's body

predator animal that hunts and kills other animals for food

survive manage to go on living

termite type of insect that lives with thousands of other termites in a huge nest

FIND OUT MORE

BOOKS

Animal (Dorling Kindersley, 2011)

Animal Encyclopedia (Dorling Kindersley, 2008)

WEBSITES

kids.nationalgeographic.co.uk/kids/animals/creaturefeature
Click on particular animals, such as earthworms, gila monsters, meerkats, and warthogs, to find out more about them.

www.bbc.co.uk/nature/adaptations/Fossorial
This website has short videos of many different burrowing animals, showing why they live in underground burrows.

www.ypte.org.uk/animal-facts.php
Find out more about many different animals on this website.

INDEX

adaptations 8, 16, 30
adapted 14, 30
American badgers 8, 9
armadillos 20–21

bears 4, 18–19
beetles 4, 5
bristles 26, 30
burrows 6, 14, 18, 22, 23, 24, 30

claws 8, 10, 12, 14, 18, 20, 21, 22
coatis 8
colonies 13

dens 18, 20
deserts 5, 7, 22, 24
dogs 28, 29

earthworms 26–27
eggs 24, 28, 29
elephants 16, 17

food, finding 6, 8, 10, 16, 17, 20

gerbils 7
gila monsters 22–23

grasslands 12, 30
grizzly bears 4

horses 28, 29

marsupials 14, 30
meerkats 6
molehills 11
moles 10–11

polar bears 18–19
pouches 14, 15
prairie dogs 12–13
predators 6, 30

scales 22
sea turtles 28, 29
spadefoot toads 24–25
survive 6, 8, 30

termites 20, 21, 30
tunnels 10, 26, 27
tusks 16–17

warthogs 16
wombats 14–15